Exploring Heritage

Ron Benson

Lynn Bryan

Kim Newlove

Charolette Player

Liz Stenson

CONSULTANTS

Susan Elliott

Diane Lomond

Ken MacInnis

Elizabeth Parchment

Contents

MOTHER MARY GREENE SCHOOL

 Selections with this symbol are available on audio.

 This symbol indicates student writing.

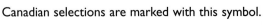 Canadian selections are marked with this symbol.

All the Colors of the Earth

by Sheila Hamanaka
Illustrated by Carmen Ngai

Children come in all the colors of the earth—
The roaring browns of bears and soaring eagles,
The whispering golds of late summer grasses,
And crackling russets of fallen leaves,
The tinkling pinks of tiny seashells by the rumbling sea.

Children come with hair like bouncy baby lambs,
Or hair that flows like water,
Or hair that curls like sleeping cats in snoozy cat colors.
Children come in all the colors of love,
In endless shades of you and me.

For love comes in cinnamon, walnut, and wheat,
Love is amber and ivory and ginger and sweet
Like caramel, and chocolate, and the honey of bees.

Dark as leopard spots, light as sand,
Children buzz with laughter that kisses our land
With sunlight like butterflies happy and free,
Children come in all the colors of the earth and sky and sea.

ABOUT THE AUTHOR

SHEILA HAMANAKA

Sheila Hamanaka grew up in New York City, where her artistic talent was encouraged by both her parents and her teachers at the High School of Music and Art. She has written and illustrated several books for children, including *The Journey* and *Screen of Frogs*. *All the Colors of the Earth* was inspired by her own two children's multi-ethnic heritage. Sheila lives in upstate New York with her daughter, Suzuko.

Tarma

by María Rosa Fort
Translated by Lori M. Carlson
and
Cynthia L. Ventura

Illustrated by Josée Masse

One afternoon late in April, which is autumn in Peru, Julian and his sister Martina were looking out at Lima's empty beaches. The wind idly blew the striped tents where, earlier in the summer, everyone changed into bathing suits, ran into the ocean, and dove into the cool and salty waters of the Pacific. Now the water was grey, empty, and uninviting. They could see the empty shores, the waves beating down tirelessly on the dark sand. "How many waves can the ocean have?" asked Julian. "How old can the ocean be?" Martina wondered.

Martina and Julian guessed at the years and counted the waves, but just when they thought they had an answer, they realized they could still hear their watches ticking and see new waves crashing on the beach. The waves seemed endless and they couldn't imagine a city without an ocean.

That afternoon Uncle Marcelo came by to pick them up from their parents' house and take them far away to spend the Easter holidays in Tarma, the small town where he had grown up. "It's up there," he said, pointing to the mountains, "way up there, higher than the city cliffs and taller than the tall buildings that line the downtown avenues." Worried that it would be a long, cold drive, Julian and Martina bundled up under layers of woollen clothes and huddled comfortably in their uncle's old car. Each chose a favorite window in the back seat and waited impatiently for the hoarse sounds of the engine to pull them out of their neighborhood streets, out of the humidity that already announced the coming winter. It was late when they finally left Lima. Martina secretly asked the sun to set later than usual so they could drive safely up the mountains and enjoy the new sights along the way.

They soon left behind the familiar city streets. Now, outside their windows, the pale walls of suburban houses started to disappear and the dust that covered everything in Lima was replaced by rocky formations of all sizes. Suddenly, a sombre river appeared on one side of the narrow road and farther ahead a cluster of fragile straw houses that seemed to bend under the weight of their television antennas. At the edge of the road, a boy with a stick in his hand was running after a skinny dog. Bushes and trees arched over the dry earth. Then Julian and Martina started to feel the mountains rise, growing steeper every minute. Soon the tall peaks enveloped them. Like a persistent worm, the car climbed the winding road up the Andes. Julian looked back and saw only mountains, more mountains, and valleys ending in darkness. The ocean was no longer there. It belonged to another world, and so did they.

Time went by slowly and they seemed to be alone on the barren soil of the Andes. Every once in a while a car or a truck would pass them, or an isolated walker would be seen steadily heading toward some hidden village behind the mountains. But for most of the drive, Uncle Marcelo's car seemed to be the only life on the silent mountains.

They finally reached the highest point on the road, where it felt as though they were at the edge of the sky, and here Martina started having the symptoms of the feared *soroche*, or altitude sickness. Julian quickly stuck some newspapers under her clothes, covering her chest with them, as his mother had suggested. Lying down in the back seat of the car, she breathed in deeply and waited for her body to get used to the dry, thin air of the Andes. The night wasn't friendly either. Darkness had set in, punctual as usual. But when the little town finally appeared in a ravine on the other side of the mountain, it was sprinkled with tiny bright lights.

Outlined by the festive bulbs were the profiles of the people of Tarma curiously examining the many strangers visiting for Holy Week.

Tarma had been invaded. Lodgings proudly displayed their no-vacancy signs. But Uncle Marcelo, Julian, and Martina soon noticed that all the private homes were open and lit, their owners unfailingly standing at the doors. It was an old tradition. Families opened their arms and houses to receive, for only a few coins, those travellers who had nowhere to spend the night. Rooms that had been closed forever were now open, forgotten beds were remade, or if need be, creaking straw mats were thrown on the floor.

Uncle Marcelo, Julian, and Martina found a place in the old house of a kind lady. The rooms were set around a stone patio. In one of them, Julian and Martina went to rest for the night. When they closed their eyes to sleep, Uncle Marcelo was still looking out the window at the town in which he was born.

Early the following morning, Julian and Martina stepped out to meet the sunny day. The clear light of the *sierra* surprised the two travellers, who were used to the grey sky of their city. They walked through the narrow, cobblestoned streets. As they arrived at the middle of the town

square, they looked up beyond the tiled roofs of the Andean town at the openness of the sky, hills, and pastures. A strange silence came over them. But Tarma soon filled up with people preparing for the main procession of Holy Week. And when they were met by their uncle, Julian and Martina joined in this mysterious ritual.

At dusk Tarma's residents and visitors from far away gathered together in the town square to chat and stroll. They talked about the next day's main event, when the women and girls of Tarma would go to gather flowers of every imaginable color. With their baskets full and their swollen aprons resting over their thickly layered skirts, they would return to the city to cover the streets with blossoms.

At sunrise the next morning the city was empty and quiet. Martina woke up early and, while everybody was still asleep, went downstairs to the patio. She crossed it, headed toward the big wooden door, and struggled to push it open. From the threshold she watched the deserted street as though she were waiting for somebody. A girl with a basket on her arm walked past her on the other side of the street. Martina followed her in silence for quite a while until they reached the end of the town, where the mountain range began. She followed her new friend down a lush green slope that ended in a gurgling stream surrounded by a bed of flowers. There they stopped. The two girls smiled at each other and knelt on the damp grass. Together they filled the basket with petals until not one more flower could fit in it. Only then could they start on their way back.

Toward noon, Tarma came to life when all the peasant girls returned from the fields with their baskets full of flowers. Bending over the uneven cobblestones of the streets, the girls began to cover them with the colorful petals. Martina watched attentively.

9

She noticed how carefully each girl's hands covered the cobblestones with designs made up of petals of every color. Uncle Marcelo had told her these were images of Holy Week. Soon the streets of Tarma were transformed.

Petals in the shape of a llama, a quino tree, a snow-capped mountain, and even a Donald Duck figure filled the streets. The cobblestones were now covered with rugs that seemed to be made out of light and velvet where all the colors of the world blended together. Martina discovered an unexpected beauty. "Hands are magical," she thought.

Meanwhile, on the other side of the sea of flowers, Uncle Marcelo and Julian were looking for Martina. They asked the barber about her, they asked the fruit vendor, the kind lady of the house, and her neighbors. But it didn't occur to them to ask the girls who had gone to the fields to pick the flowers. They finally found Martina near the square looking at the peaceful, flowered streets.

Soon dusk was ready to fall upon the town. Uncle Marcelo, Julian, and Martina stayed together to watch the procession.

When the last rays of the sun flooded the central nave of the Cathedral, the leader of the procession gave a signal to the faithful gathered inside it. They bent their knees slightly to place on their shoulders the heavy wooden platform bearing the statue of Jesus. The members of the procession timed their steps to the rhythm of drumbeats and trumpets. Behind them the people of Tarma and the many visitors accompanied the sacred images on their slow journey through the town. As the people advanced, the delicate petals died one by one. Absorbed by the drama of the procession, Martina looked at the peasant girl's hands now folded in prayer.

For hours, while the green fields around Tarma darkened with the setting sun, the faithful continued to walk on the flowers of Tarma. The procession wound along the streets and then back inside the cathedral lit with the flickering of innumerable candles.

The celebrations were over. In the town that night, everyone dreamed quiet dreams while outside the wind swept away the last traces of the llama, the tree, the mountain, the duck. The house of the kind lady was now dark. Everybody was asleep. Across the room, Martina heard Julian breathing deeply. She closed her eyes, and when everything around her disappeared behind the smell of her alpaca blanket, she said goodbye to Tarma. As she fell asleep, she could already feel the slow whirl taking her down the tall mountains toward the foot of the Andes. And further, down to the ocean, where the waves still crashed on the dark sands of Lima.

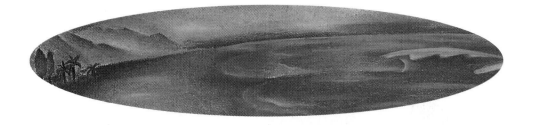

Cat's Cradle

by Camilla Gryski
Illustrated by Allan Moon

Cat's cradles, or string figures, are designs you weave on your fingers with a loop of string.

We don't know when people first started playing with string, or which people invented this ancient art. We do know that all early societies had and used string—for hunting, fishing, and weaving—and that string figures have been collected from Native Peoples all over the world.

The Inuit, for example, create some of the most complicated and beautiful string figures ever recorded. And because string figures are known throughout the world, from south-east Asia and Japan to South America and the Caribbean, they continue to come to Canada with newcomers from many lands.

Making string figures was a pastime and an art. The string artist was often a storyteller as well, using his loop of string to illustrate his tale. The string figures were of animals or stars or other things from nature. Some figures moved and some were like magic.

Share these figures with your friends. Maybe they can show you some new ones. You can experiment too; you may invent something wonderful.

And remember: always carry a string in your pocket!

Anthropologists used to be described as people with their pockets full of string.

About Loops

When the string goes around your finger or thumb, it makes a **loop**.

The loops take their names from their location on your hands: **thumb loop, index loop, middle finger loop, ring finger loop, little finger loop**.

If you move a loop from one finger to another, it gets a new name: a loop that was on your thumb but is now on your little finger is a new little finger loop.

Each loop has a **near string**—the one nearer (or closer) to you—and a **far string**—the one farther from you.

If there are two loops on your thumb or finger, one is the **lower loop**—the one near the base of your thumb or finger—and the other is the **upper loop**—the one near the top of your thumb or finger. Don't get these loops mixed up, and be sure to keep them apart.

About Making the Figures

As you make the following figures, you will be weaving the strings of the loops on your fingers. Your fingers or thumbs can go over or under the strings to pick up one or more strings, then go back to the basic position.

Sometimes you may **drop** or **release** a loop from your fingers.

It takes a little while to get used to holding your hands so that the strings don't drop off your fingers. If you accidentally drop a loop or a string, it is best to start all over again.

Now go and get your string—let's begin!

Names of the Strings

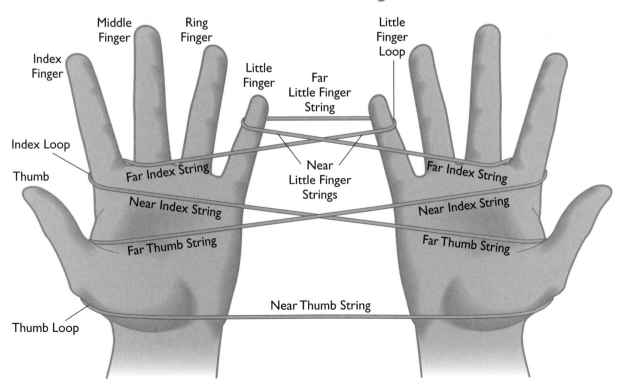

The Basic Position

*Your hands begin in the **basic position** for most string figures and usually return to the basic position after each move.*

1. Your hands are parallel, the palms are facing each other, and your fingers are pointing up.

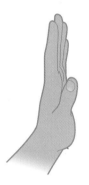

The hands in some of the pictures are not in the basic position. The hands are shown with the palms facing you so that you can see all the strings clearly.

Position 1

1. With your hands in the basic position, hang the loop of string on your thumbs. Stretch your hands as far apart as you can, to make the string loop tight.

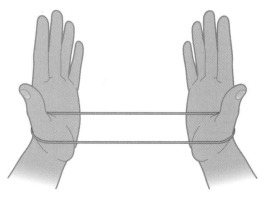

2. Pick up the far thumb string with your little fingers. The string that goes across the palm of your hand is called the **palmar string**.

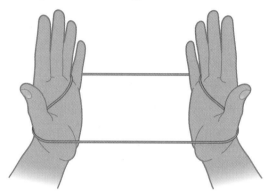

The Twitcher

This string figure originally came from the South Pacific. In some places, it was called Mrs. Crab. You'll have to use your imagination to see Mrs. Crab walking along. In Hawaii it was called the Twitcher, but when it travelled to Japan, it became known as the Elastic Band.

Double your long string or use a short loop for this figure.

1. Do Position 1.

2. Your fingers are pointing up. Point them away from you. Now your thumbs are pointing up and the string loop has a top string and a bottom string.

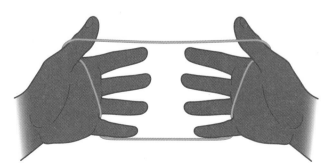

3. Slide your hands along the string loop until your thumbs touch the bottom string. Now your thumbs are pointing down. Move your fingers sideways towards each other until your hands look exactly like the ones in the picture.

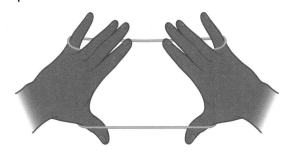

4. Catch the bottom string on the backs of your thumbs and return your hands to the basic position. Now your fingers are pointing up and there are loops on your thumbs and little fingers.

5. Your thumbs get the near little finger string and return.

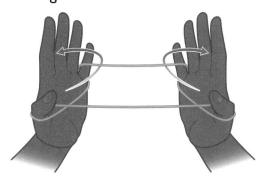

6. Your little fingers get the far thumb string and return.

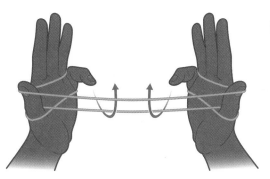

7. From above, put your index fingers down into the loops between your little fingers and thumbs, and on their backs, pick up the front palmar strings.

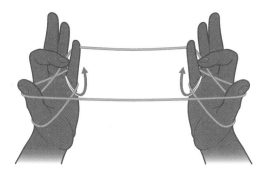

8. Tip your thumbs down (or use your mouth), to let the upper straight thumb string slide off your thumbs.

9. Tip your little fingers down (or use your mouth), to let the upper straight little finger string slide off your little fingers.

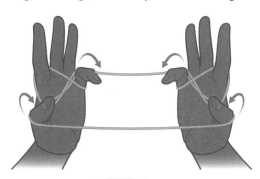

How to Make the Twitcher Twitch or the Elastic Band Stretch

10. Stretch your fingers apart and your hands will move close together.

11. Now let your fingers collapse and pull your hands apart.

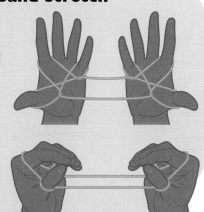

The Fish Spear

This string figure represented a fish spear or harpoon to the people who lived in the Torres Straits between Australia and New Guinea, a duck spear in Alaska, and a coconut palm tree in Africa. The Salish people call it Pitching a Tent.

1. Do Position 1.

2. Your right index finger goes under the left palmar string and pulls it out a little bit.

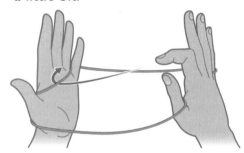

3. Your right index finger **twists its loop**. (See instructions below on How to Twist a Loop.)

How to Twist a Loop

Rotate your index finger away from you, down, towards you, and up. Make sure the twist is in the string loop, not around your index finger.

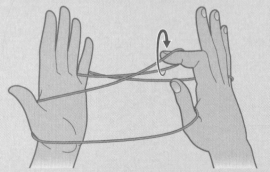

Do it again. There are now two twists in the strings of the right index loop.

4. Your right index finger pulls out its twisted loop as far as it will go.

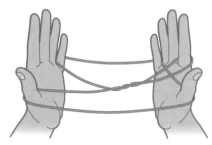

5. Your left index finger picks up, from below, the right palmar string between the strings of the right index loop. Now pull this loop out as far as it will go.

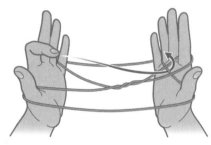

6. Your right thumb and right little finger drop their loops. Pull your right index finger out as far as it will go so that the loops move up the string towards your left hand. Now you've made the Fish Spear.

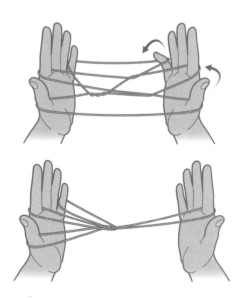

A Children's Chorus

Celebrating the Thirtieth Anniversary of the Declaration of the Rights of the Child

Introduction

All children have rights: the right to protection, to education, to food and medical care, and to much more.

Every child, no matter where he or she lives, has the right to grow up feeling safe and cared for: a simple thought, which few would openly challenge.

But, sadly, the reality is quite different.

Every day children are born who are denied rights. Some are victims of violence, poverty, and abuse. Many are exploited. Many cannot even grow up with their own families because their countries are ravaged by war. Some go hungry because there is famine; others will never have the chance to learn and grow; some cannot even play.

This selection is about the Rights of the Child: for children to look at, to share with a brother or sister, parent, teacher, or friend.

Audrey Hepburn
UNICEF Goodwill Ambassador

Principle One: We are the children of the world. No matter who our parents are, where we live, or what we believe, treat us as equals. We deserve the best the world has to give.

Principle Two: Protect us, so that we may grow in freedom and with dignity.

Principle Three: Let us each be given a name, and have a land to call our own.

Principle Four: Keep us warm and sheltered. Give us food to eat and a place to play. If we are sick, nurse and comfort us.

Principle Five: If we are developmentally or physically challenged, treasure us even more and meet our special needs.

Principle Six: Let us grow up in a family. If we cannot be cared for by our own family, take us in and love us just the same.

Principle Seven: Teach us well, so that we may lead happy and useful lives. But let us play, so that we may also teach ourselves.

Principle Eight: In times of trouble, help us among the first. The future of the world depends on us.

Principle Nine: Protect us from cruelty and from those who hurt and abuse us.

Principle Ten: Raise us with respect for equity and diversity, freedom, and love. As we grow up, we, too, will promote peace and understanding throughout the world.

Declaration of the Rights of the Child
as unanimously adopted by the General Assembly of the United Nations on November 20, 1959

PREAMBLE

Whereas the peoples of the United Nations have, in the Charter, reaffirmed their faith in fundamental human rights, and in the dignity and worth of the human person, and have determined to promote social progress and better standards of life in larger freedom.

Whereas the United Nations has, in the Universal Declaration of Human Rights, proclaimed that everyone is entitled to all the rights and freedoms set forth therein, without distinction of any kind, such as race, color, sex, language, religion, political or other opinion, national or social origin, property, birth, or other status.

Whereas the child, by reason of his physical and mental immaturity, needs special safeguards and care, including appropriate legal protection, before as well as after birth.

Whereas the need for such special safeguards has been stated in the General Declaration of the Rights of the Child of 1924, and recognized in the Universal Declaration of Human Rights and in the statutes of specialized agencies and international organizations concerned with the welfare of children.

Whereas mankind owes to the child the best it has to give.

Now therefore,
The General Assembly
Proclaims this
Declaration of the Rights of the Child to the end that he may have a happy childhood and enjoy for his own good and for the good of society the rights and freedoms herein set forth, and calls upon parents, upon men and women as individuals, and upon voluntary organizations, local authorities, and national Governments to recognize these rights and strive for their observance by legislative and other measures progressively taken in accordance with the following principles:

PRINCIPLE 1 The child shall enjoy all the rights set forth in this Declaration. All children, without any exception whatsoever, shall be entitled to these rights, without distinction or discrimination on account of race, color, sex, language, religion, political or other opinion, national or social origin, property, birth, or other status, whether of himself or of his family.

PRINCIPLE 2 The child shall enjoy special protection, and shall be given opportunities and facilities, by law and by other means, to enable him to develop physically, mentally, morally, spiritually, and socially in a healthy and normal manner and in conditions of freedom and dignity. In the enactment of laws for this purpose the best interests of the child shall be the paramount consideration.

PRINCIPLE 3 The child shall be entitled from his birth to a name and nationality.

PRINCIPLE 4 The child shall enjoy the benefits of social security. He shall be entitled to grow and develop in health: to this end special care and protection shall be provided both to him and to his mother, including adequate prenatal and postnatal care. The child shall have the right to adequate nutrition, housing, recreation, and medical services.

PRINCIPLE 5 The child who is physically, mentally, or socially challenged shall be given the special treatment, education, and care required by his particular condition.

PRINCIPLE 6 The child, for the full and harmonious development of his personality, needs love and understanding. He shall, wherever possible, grow up in the care and under the responsibility of his parents, and in any case in an atmosphere of affection and of moral and material security; a child of tender years shall not, save in exceptional circumstances, be separated from his mother. Society and the public authorities shall have the duty to extend particular care to children without a family and those without adequate means of support. Payment of state and other assistance toward the maintenance of children of large families is desirable.

PRINCIPLE 7 The child is entitled to receive education, which shall be free and compulsory, at least in the elementary stages. He shall be given an education which will promote his general culture, and enable him on a basis of equal opportunity to develop his abilities, his individual judgement, and his sense of moral and social responsibility, and to become a useful member of society.

The best interests of the child shall be the guiding principle of those responsible for his education and guidance; that responsibility lies in the first place with his parents.

The child shall have full opportunity for play and recreation, which should be directed to the same purpose as education; society and the public authorities shall endeavor to promote the enjoyment of this right.

PRINCIPLE 8 The child shall in all circumstances be among the first to receive protection and relief.

PRINCIPLE 9 The child shall be protected against all forms of neglect, cruelty, and exploitation. He shall not be the subject of traffic, in any form.

The child shall not be admitted to employment before an appropriate minimum age; he shall in no case be caused or permitted to engage in any occupation or employment which would prejudice his health or education, or interfere with his physical, mental, or moral development.

PRINCIPLE 10 The child shall be protected from practices which may foster racial, religious, and any other form of discrimination. He shall be brought up in a spirit of understanding, tolerance, friendship among peoples, peace, and universal brotherhood and in full consciousness that his energy and talents should be devoted to the service of his fellow men.

2x2x2x2x2x2x2

Everybody has two parents, four grandparents, and eight great-grandparents. Believe it or not, you have 1024 great-great-great-great-great-great-great-great-grandparents. Hence the title "2x2x2x2x2x2x2."

If all this is true, then somewhere down the line you may be related to the person sitting next to you in class, your next-door neighbor, and someone living halfway across the world. You may be related to all the famous people of the world, Albert Einstein, the star on your favorite TV show—even royalty, like Queen Elizabeth. Though you may not be directly related, somewhere down the timeline, you may be related to everybody.

Genna Evelyn
Age 12

This story was inspired by a question in my school math book about the powers of 2. Since then, I've been wondering how far back we'd have to go before we became related to everybody in our city.

Genna Evelyn

Different People

There are a lot of different people in the world.
Some are young and some are old.
Some are tall and some are short.
Some like to even laugh and snort.
Some have blond hair, some have brown.
Some cry and put on a frown.
Some like the colors black and white.
Some like fluorescent yellow that's really bright.
Some people's faces are oval or round.
Some have white skin, some have brown.
Some are Italian and some are Spanish.
Some are French and some are English.
Some eyes are blue, and some are brown.
Some are green and they may be round.
Some like cats, and some like dogs.
Some collect cards, and some collect pogs.

We all are different in a lot of special ways.
But in one way we are all the same: we all are human beings.
So I choose people for what they are like in the inside, not from the outside.

Holly Bedo
Age 12

How People Are Alike and Different Around the World

People all around the world are alike. Almost everybody has two eyes to see, two ears to hear, one nose to smell, one mouth to speak, two arms to move, two legs to walk, and a functional body. Mostly everybody has five fingers on each hand and five toes on each foot. Almost everybody has a brain to learn and make mistakes.

People all around the world are different. Almost everybody has a different color of hair, eye color, weight, and body size. Almost everybody has different ways of learning to have different habits and different attitudes. Every person from a certain country may have different languages, cultures, and beliefs.

Conrad Siu
Grade 5

21

Tides of Change

Faces of the Northwest Coast

by Sheryl McFarlane
Illustrated by Ken Campbell

Do you know the Northwest Coast? Do you know her many histories?

Petroglyphs carved into stone by ancient peoples are doorways to ten thousand years of past.

Ship logs and charts reveal exploration routes. But do they tell of the hopes and fears of sailors who sought gold and furs and a fabled sea-link to the Orient?

It's hard to imagine that the name on a weathered gravestone once belonged to a child who skipped and sang and played as you do now.

Solitary lighthouse keepers have signalled the dangers of coastal waterways for more than a century. And when the fog rolls in so thick it's like a wall, passing ships are still thankful for the blast of invisible foghorns.

The rough-and-ready lumberjacks of yesterday measured giant Sitka Spruce and Douglas Fir in board feet and the time it took to fall them with sweat and two-man saws.

When you peer through the sagging doorways of a deserted coastal town, can you hear the cry of "GOLD," or was that just the wind whistling through the trees?

Have you seen kayakers challenging the sea? This coast has sparked the spirit of adventure many times before. Names like Quadra, Cook, Bering, and Vancouver ring out along northwest shores.

Do you know the Northwest Coast? Do you know her people?

Have you met artists carving windows into their culture with every new totem pole they raise?

On chilly winter mornings before first light has touched the bay, the lowest yearly tides announce the beginning of the clam diggers' day.

Do you know rubber-booted cannery workers, bone-weary when the sun is sinking low and one last fishboat is still unloading at the docks?

Have you seen the children of isolated shores and windswept islands waiting for the schoolboat in the early morning drizzle?

Or known the anxious families of a troller crew forced to wait out a sudden summer storm in a distant cove?

You've seen tugs towing ships a hundred times their size, but not the taut muscles of the skipper's jaw. Once safely through the churning narrows, he shares a grin with his daughter, a third-generation tug captain in the making.

Walk past downtown docks to Chinatown with its bustling market stalls, narrow streets, and crowded shops. The dragons that twist and writhe on doorways, signs, and kites recall ancient mythologies to life.

Do you know the Northwest Coast? Do you know the many faces of her beauty?

Have you walked along a beach wiped clean like an empty slate? Your footprints are as fleeting as the shifting dunes of sand rising in the distance.

Imagine water spraying skyscraper-high when a wall of ice breaks free and crashes into the ocean. The glacier's chill will make you shiver even on a twenty-hour summer day.

Have you watched a dozen sea lions at play in the frothy water or seen their frantic rush to reach the shore when a pod of transient orcas surfaces too near?

You could lose an afternoon exploring tidepool treasures, where fascinating worlds in miniature are daily nourished by the sea.

Climb the rocky bluffs to watch Grey Whales pass on one of the longest migrations of any mammal known. Whalers called them devilfish long ago. But those who reach out to touch their barnacle-encrusted skin know them now as the gentle giants.

Follow the banks of a river teeming with the struggles of spawning salmon. Have you ever wondered how they find their way from the open sea? Or how bald eagles seem to know exactly when to be there waiting for their yearly salmon feast?

Old growth coastal forests touched by a hundred thousand days of mist and rain have existed for an eternity. Yet we've only just begun to understand the intricacy of this living tapestry.

Do you know the Northwest Coast?
Have you seen the tides of change that have swept her shores and touched her people?

Will you shape her future, or will her winds and tides and waves shape yours?

Author's Notes

Radiocarbon dating is an important tool for estimating the age of very old objects. But, it's no help for dating petroglyphs since they contain no carbon. One petroglyph depicting a paddlewheel steamer must have been carved after 1836, the year the first paddle steamer arrived on the Northwest coast. A reliable means of dating petroglyphs has not yet been discovered.

The **Nuu-chah-nulth** version of Captain Cook's first visit to Vancouver Island in 1778 is very different from the one most history books have recorded. Long ago the people of Yuquot were surprised by two strange ships. They welcomed the strangers by leading them to safety. The villagers cried, "nu•tka•ʔičim ("go around the point"). The strangers thought the villagers were introducing themselves as Nootka. The Nuu-chah-nulth people have been wrongly called Nootka Indians ever since.

Today, a cough might keep you home from school for a few days. But before the introduction of antibiotics and immunizations, **whooping cough (pertussis)** was only one of many illnesses that caused the deaths of thousands of children each year.

In 1906, **Minnie Patterson**, wife of the Cape Beale Lighthouse keeper, made headlines for her heroic, four-hour ordeal to get help for the crew of a sinking ship during a storm. She was awarded a medal, but most keepers and their families remain unknown and unsung heroes.

Before the days of chainsaws, some trees could take hand-loggers an entire day to take down. The remains of **springboards** can still sometimes be found embedded in tree stumps. These narrow platforms were used to raise the loggers above the butt-swell of the tree, reducing the amount of wood they had to cut through.

In 1896, Skagua (now Skagway, Alaska) was an isolated Tlingit village. In two years, it grew to more than 20 000 people. At its peak, the town boasted 19 restaurants, 15 general stores, and 4 newspapers. A few years later, its population plunged to less than 500. Why? The **Klondike Gold Rush** had come and gone!

Today, most kayaks are made from modern materials such as fibreglass or kevlar. But, their basic design has not changed from the **closed-skin boats** Aleutian whale hunters relied on for thousands of years. Aleutians even had their own version of waterproof jackets, or **kamleikas**. These were made by carefully stitching together strips of sea lion or walrus intestines.

Since the earliest carvers had no hard metals, the first **totem poles** were carved using blades made out of sharpened shells, stone, or bone and often took many years to complete.

Clams belong to a huge group of two-shelled animals called bivalves. Not all clams are harmless. **Toredos** or **shipworms** are very destructive wood-boring clams. The shells of these worm-like animals do not house them, but are modified raspers for tunnelling through wood.

Today, most of us take canned food for granted. But, scientists believe that lead poisoning from canned food may have helped to doom the famous **Franklin Expedition** of 1845. The body of one crew member was exhumed and tested for lead poisoning in 1986. They found more than enough lead to have caused his death.

Much of the Northwest coast is either too rugged or too isolated to be accessible by land. Instead of cars, people in these communities rely on boats to get around, including **school boats**!

A fishboat is a fishboat is a fishboat. Right? Wrong! **Trollers** trail fish lines suspended from rigging, while **seiners** rely on a vertical net wall to trap their catch. Sheets of netting are dropped into the water with floats at the top and weights at the bottom. Fish are scooped up by pulling the bottom of the net up and in. **Gillnetters** are a whole other story!

The first tugs were really passenger and freighter steamships like the *Beaver*. They sometimes pulled a tow because they were the only power boats around.

Chinese immigrants brought a rich and vastly different cultural heritage to their new homes on the Northwest Coast. Traditions like the Dragon Dance attract thousands. Unlike the feared, fire-breathing dragons of European folklore, Chinese **cloud-breathing dragons** are revered. They are associated with strength, renewal, and good fortune.

What is not alive but is constantly on the move? Sand dunes! Tough **dunegrass, sedge**, and **beach pines** help to stabilize most coastal dunes. Dunegrass was also widely used by several Northwest coast tribes for a variety of woven articles.

Have you ever wondered why glaciers seem to look blue? It all has to do with snow! It's probably no surprise that snow is 90% air. The other 10% is delicate, star-shaped crystals of frozen water vapor. The snow at the bottom of a glacier has had most of the air squeezed out from between these crystals, so it reflects mainly blue light. Scientists have given the name **blue ice** to this very dense glacial snow. Since icebergs break, or **calve**, off glaciers, they also contain blue ice.

The Northwest coast is home to two types of orcas or killer whales. **Transients** and **residents** are different in almost every way. Residents are found in the same places at the same times, year after year. They live in large pods of up to fifty whales, and tend to rely mainly on a diet of fish. Transients travel alone or in small pods of less than six and feed primarily on marine mammals such as sea lions. Their migration patterns remain a mystery.

Purple sea stars may be common, but some of their adaptations are most unusual! They can regrow lost arms—handy if you have a twenty-year lifespan. And it's a good thing they don't need shoes for their thousand-plus tube-like feet. Stranger still—their idea of dining out is to push their own stomach into their prey's shell, where it digests its meal before returning home!

Grey whales are infected with a unique **barnacle** larvae just after birth. Once attached to the whale's blubber, these freeloading filter feeders are guaranteed a constant food supply. They travel with the whales on an annual 15 000- to 18 000-kilometre migration from Baja, Mexico, to the Bering or Chukchi Seas and back again. It will be the only home these barnacles will ever know, and if the whale dies, the barnacles die with it.

One short stretch of the Chilkat River in Alaska has been known to attract as many as 3495 **bald eagles** during salmon spawning season. But, in 1994, an astounding 3766 bald eagles were recorded at a site on the Squamish River in British Columbia!

Imagine a tree as tall as a thirty-storey building. Just such a tree—a ninety-five-metre **Sitka spruce**—is the largest of its kind in the world. It can be found towering above its Carmanah Valley neighbors on Vancouver Island in British Columbia.

ABOUT THE AUTHOR

SHERYL McFARLANE

Sheryl McFarlane is the author of several successful books, including *Waiting for the Whales*, which won the Governor General's Literary Award for illustration. Sheryl says that when she was young she never imagined herself as a writer, but "once I began writing, I knew that it was what I most wanted to do." Currently at work on more stories, she is also enjoying her family, gardening, biking, and lots of reading. She lives with her husband and three children in Victoria, British Columbia.

Heroine of Lunenburg

by Joyce Barkhouse
Illustrated by Peter Ferguson

Sylvia posed in front of the long mirror in Colonel Creighton's parlor. Tall and slim, with skin like polished ebony, she couldn't help smiling at her reflection. As she dropped herself a curtsy and spun around, the great skirt of her beautiful green silk gown billowed out like the sails of a ship.

Clapping her hands, Sylvia laughed out loud with pleasure.

Abruptly her delight ended as she heard the sound of heavy footsteps. Then a wheezy voice exclaimed,

"What's going on here? Where did you get that gown?"

Sylvia whirled to face the short, stout woman who came into the room with a small, fair-haired boy.

"It's mine, Missy Smith! The gown is mine! Mistress Creighton gave it to me afore she died," Sylvia cried.

"You're lying! You're a thief," Mistress shouted, her tiny eyes blazing with anger.

"Sylvie's not a liar! Mamma did give her the green dress!" cried the boy angrily, running to Sylvia's side. "And she's not a thief, either."

"She's a black slave, that's what she is, and she's no business in the parlor," retorted the woman.

The boy stamped his foot and burst into tears.

"I hate you! You're mean," he cried.

"That's enough, Master Timmy! Come along at once. As for you, Sylvia, get downstairs to the kitchen where you belong. Colonel Creighton will hear about this."

So saying, Mistress Smith seized Timmy by the arm and dragged him from the room. For a minute Sylvia stayed defiantly where she was.

Then, instead of going to the kitchen, she slipped into the garden and ran to a favorite corner by the picket fence, where she was hidden from the house by a clump of lilac bushes. For a long time she remained there, sad and brooding.

The home of Colonel Creighton stood on the slope of a steep hill overlooking Lunenburg harbor, on the south shore of Nova Scotia. From her hiding place Sylvia could see over the roofs of the closely clustered houses to the harbor itself. It was empty of ships that day, for the men of the town had set sail for deep-sea fishing off the Grand Banks of Newfoundland.

Suddenly a shiver ran through Sylvia and she felt a strange sense of foreboding. It was midsummer of the year 1782, a year when England was at war with her rebellious colonies to the south. No coastal settlement in Nova Scotia was ever entirely safe from the looting, pillaging, and burning of Yankee privateers. Sylvia looked away from the harbor and out to sea, but there were no ships there. All seemed safe and peaceful.

"It's just 'cause I'm upset, seeing Timmy crying all the time and not being able to go and comfort him," she decided, trying to shake off her uneasiness. Turning her back on the sea, she peered through the lilacs at the Creighton house.

"Missy Creighton wouldn't like what's happening," she murmured sadly. "Not to Timmy nor to me."

Sylvia thought about all the things that had changed since Mrs. Creighton's death and especially since Timmy's fifth birthday a few months ago.

"Timmy needs a governess, someone to teach him his lessons and proper manners," Colonel Creighton had announced.

The choice of Mistress Smith to fill the post had not been a happy one. Unfortunately, English-speaking servants were hard to find in an outpost like Lunenburg. Except for Colonel Creighton's household and the handful of soldiers at the blockhouse, almost all the town's inhabitants spoke German.

"Wish I could have taught Timmy to read and write and cipher," Sylvia sighed. But, like most slaves, she had been denied the opportunity to learn such things herself.

Sylvia looked again at the flowing skirt of the green silk dress and smoothed the lovely material with her hands. Tears came to her eyes as she remembered the morning her mistress had called her to her bedside.

"Sylvia, we both know that I haven't much longer to live," Mrs. Creighton had said. "I want to tell you how grateful I am that you've been with me all these years. You're the best friend I've had in this wild country, and I know that Timmy will never want for mothering as long as you're with him. Now I want you to look in my closet and choose one of my party dresses—perhaps that green one, with the gold braid, that you've admired so much. Keep it for your own and dress up in it sometimes. It will help you remember the happy times we've had together—you and Timmy and I."

At first Sylvia had cried and had not wanted to take the dress, but now she was glad she had. She knew she should never wear the dress in front of Colonel Creighton, but sometimes she put it on when she was alone or with Timmy, just for fun.

Sylvia smoothed the dress again and got slowly to her feet.

"I must change and get back to work," she said. But when she reached the lean-to that served as her sleeping and dressing room, she found her bundle of garments had disappeared.

She hurried into the kitchen. Mistress Smith was there, poking at something in the fireplace. A rank odor filled the air.

"What are you doing?" cried Sylvia in dismay, as she recognized the smell of burning cloth.

"Since you have such a fine gown, I thought you'd have no need for your old rags. I've burned them," came the reply.

"But that's wicked! I have no other clothes!" cried Sylvia.

"Then you'll just have to wear what you have on, won't you?" Mistress Smith said, with a cruel smile, as she left the room.

Bitterly, Sylvia went about her evening tasks. She tried to move carefully around the small kitchen but she was hampered by the great billowing skirt. She brushed it against the greasy edge of the slab table, spattered gravy on it from the roast, and dipped the hem into the hot ashes as she lifted the kettle from the hob. Already the gown—the only beautiful thing she had ever owned—was ruined.

That night she cried herself to sleep. She slept uneasily, awakening before anyone else was about, to hear the first cock crow in the early dawn. Immediately her thoughts turned to what she could wear. She thought of going to Colonel Creighton for help, but she knew it would be of little use. Mistress Smith would already have given him her version of the story. In desperation, she tried wrapping herself in the blanket that covered her straw mattress, but she realized at once she could never clutch it about her as she worked. Sorrowfully, she pulled on the soiled green dress again.

She built up the fire in the kitchen, carried water from the well, and set it to boil. Next she had to go to the far pasture with the milking stool and bucket to milk the cows. Getting away from the house felt good. For a little while she could pretend she was free, free as the white gulls that swooped and soared over the sea.

As she walked high up on the hill, though, she felt again the same unease she had known the previous evening. This time she made no attempt to put it from her but instead breathed deeply, moving her head from side to side. Could there be a bear or wildcat among the cattle, she wondered? But no, her sixth sense told her that if indeed there were danger about, it came from elsewhere.

She stopped to stand and listen. A song sparrow trilled and a whiff of wood smoke, mixed with the sweet perfume of wild roses, came to her. Then somehow the world seemed unnaturally still. She entered the pasture. Now she was sure there was something wrong. The cattle had stopped in their grazing. Every one of them was staring out to sea. She followed their gaze.

Down in the harbor a boat was coming swiftly to shore as men bent strongly to their oars. Beyond it, a tall vessel rode at anchor. The banner at the vessel's masthead was not the Jack of England. Privateers!

Clutching stool and bucket, kicking at the green dress as it caught and twisted around her legs, Sylvia raced down the hill.

"Master! The Yankees are coming!" she gasped, as she burst into the house where the family sat at breakfast.

Colonel Creighton strode to the window.

"Get my gun from the kitchen. I must go to the blockhouse," he ordered sharply, as he buckled on his sword.

Sylvia obeyed, and then stood in the doorway to watch her master go. Even as she watched, armed men came rushing up the hill and the first shot was fired. Behind her, Mistress Smith uttered a wild scream. Numb with shock, Sylvia could neither move nor think till Timmy pushed past her and ran outside.

"No! No, Timmy," she cried.

A warning bullet whistled past her head. Forgetting all else she ran down the steps, gathered the boy in her arms and threw herself on the ground, shielding his body with her own. Moments later she looked up and saw that men were smashing windows and doors in a nearby house.

"Let us in! Or we'll set your place afire!" they shouted. A woman shouted something back at them in German. Sylvia's mind began to work again.

"Hush, Timmy," she whispered. "Don't cry. We must try to save what we can."

Her dress was torn now, and covered with dust, but she gave it no thought. Gathering up the skirts as best she could and taking Timmy's hand, she went back into the house and snatched her empty milk bucket from the floor.

"Stay here, Tim," she said, pushing the little boy under a table for safety.

Mistress Smith and the other servants had disappeared. Alone then, Sylvia fetched Colonel Creighton's strong box. She dropped it inside the bucket and carried it outside. To her relief no one was watching. Quickly she lowered the bucket into the well and hurried back to the house.

All around now the town was in an uproar. People were streaming out of their homes towards the surrounding woods, some running empty-handed, others staggering under pieces of furniture. Sounds of gunfire came from the blockhouse.

Timmy had stayed under the table.

"Come on, now. Let's get the chest of silver outside," Sylvia said.

She had dragged the heavy box only halfway across the garden when a group of privateers came around the corner of the house. Quick as a flash she saw that she could profit now from Mistress Smith's cruelty of the day before. Holding Timmy in her arms she sank down, covering the chest with her flowing skirts. One of the men went up to her.

"Why haven't you run off to the woods with the others?" he roared.

Seizing her by one arm he yanked at her viciously. She resisted, screaming at the top of her lungs. Terrified, Timmy pounded at the privateer with his fists.

"Leave her alone! Leave her alone!" he cried.

Another man joined them.

"Orders have just been issued not to burn any more buildings," he directed. "Get what valuables you can from here, and move on."

The men left. Sylvia dragged the chest across the grassy lawn and hid it in the lilac bushes. Then, at last, she and Timmy ran up the hill and through the pasture to the shelter of the forest.

Before dark the privateers sailed away. From her lookout Sylvia could see that Colonel Creighton's house remained standing, and nearly all the fires had burned low.

"Come on, Timmy. Let's go home," she said.

That night she slept alone with Timmy in her arms. "Don't be afraid," she comforted him.

"I'm not scared when I'm with you, Sylvia," he whispered. "But where is Papa?"

"I don't know," she had to say.

Others came back to the ruined town next day, but Colonel Creighton did not return. When a relief ship sailed in days later, from Halifax, Sylvia learned that he and two other men had given themselves up as hostages to prevent the whole town being razed.

Mistress Smith took ship at once for Halifax. The other servants followed her example but Sylvia refused to leave. Since no one else seemed to care about Timmy, she kept him with her.

It was the beginning of a free and happy time for both of them. They picked wild berries and gathered nuts. They had milk in plenty, some of which Sylvia made into butter and cheese. The hens laid well so there were eggs to trade and sell as well as to eat. What's more, Sylvia made friends with some neighboring Micmac. They brought gifts of meat—hare and partridge and venison—in return for loaves of bread and scalding hot cups of strong tea.

Colonel Creighton knew none of this. When, in 1783, at the end of the war, he was released, no one could tell him what had become of his only son. Broken-hearted and believing himself to be ruined, he returned to Lunenburg simply to salvage what he could. As he climbed the hill, he was both surprised and angry to see smoke rising from the chimney of his home.

"Squatters!" he thought. "Someone has moved in, thinking I'd never come back."

When he opened the door, though, he was greeted by a glad cry. Timmy, rosy cheeked and well, threw himself into his

father's arms. Stunned with surprise, the Colonel looked up to see Sylvia's welcoming smile.

"I—I can't believe it," he said, tears of gratitude filling his eyes.

It was Timmy who told the story of Sylvia's courage, and who showed his father where the strong box and chest of silver had been buried behind the lilac bushes in the garden.

Everything was there, down to the smallest coin. As the Colonel again tried to express his thanks, Sylvia grinned.

"It was lucky, after all, I was wearing Missy Creighton's green gown. Remember? My own skimpy skirt would never have covered that chest," she said.

Somewhat ashamed, she looked down at the ragged makeshift dress she had sewed together from scraps of cloth.

"You'll never want for proper clothing again," Colonel Creighton declared indignantly. "Tomorrow we pack and get ready to return to Halifax, for I'm no longer posted here."

And so it was Sylvia left Lunenburg for good. For a few years she remained with Colonel Creighton and Timmy, but it was of her own choice, for the Colonel wasted no time in signing legal papers that freed her from slavery.

In Halifax, she met and fell in love with another freed slave. They were married and there the record of Sylvia's life ends. It is, however, likely that she and her husband settled in one of Nova Scotia's Black Loyalist communities. Certainly the story of her strength and loyalty, her honesty and courage, should live on forever.

ABOUT THE AUTHOR JOYCE BARKHOUSE

Joyce Barkhouse is a former school teacher who began writing short fiction for children in the 1930s. However, she did not publish her first book until she was sixty-one. Her short stories have appeared in several textbooks, story collections, and teachers' magazines. She won the first Ann Connor-Brimer Award for outstanding contribution to children's literature in Atlantic Canada for *Pit Pony*, which also was shortlisted for three other awards. Her most recent book is called *Smallest Rabbit*.

From
Waterways (to) Airways

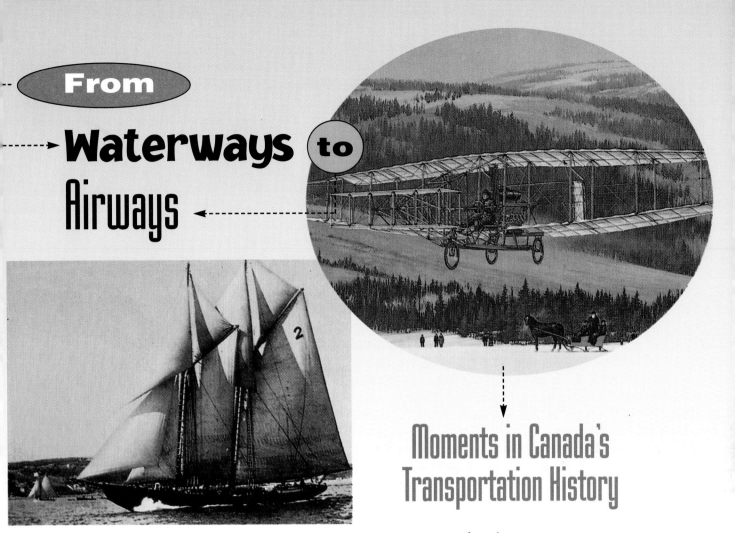

Moments in Canada's Transportation History

by Liz Stenson

From the earliest times, getting from place to place in Canada has been a challenge.

One reason is distance. From Cape Spear, Newfoundland, on the Atlantic coast, to Beaver Creek, Yukon, on the Pacific coast, Canada stretches for over 5000 kilometres. If you were to go from Alert, on Ellesmere Island in the north, to Point Pelee in the south, you would need to travel over 4600 kilometres. Canada is a vast land, the second-largest country in the world.

Our country also has towering mountains, great plains, dense forests, grassy fields, sparse tundra, and millions of lakes and rivers. Even today, much of it is still wilderness. In such a large and diverse country, with great distances between communities, good transportation has always been very important. In fact, the history of Canada is strongly linked to the history of its transportation.

Today, fast jets whisk people across the country in a matter of hours. Modern highways and rail lines link almost every community in the country. Large freighters carry goods through the Great Lakes and the St. Lawrence Seaway to the Atlantic Ocean.

But it wasn't always this way. . . .

Canada is a land of water, from coastal seas to great lakes to swiftly flowing rivers and streams. Long before the Europeans arrived, the Aboriginal Peoples had discovered that these waterways provided the most efficient way to travel.

Aboriginal Peoples in many parts of the country found that the canoe provided an ideal method of transportation. No other type of water transportation has played such an important role in our history.

▲ **The birchbark canoe.**
The Woodland Peoples, who lived in the forest, made their canoes out of birchbark fastened to a wooden frame. The bark of the birch tree made excellent building material. It was readily available, light, tough, and waterproof. It could be stripped away without killing the tree, so there was always a fresh supply.

The birchbark canoe was easy to control, and was ideal for navigating narrow streams and rushing rapids, or crossing large lakes. Its light weight made it ideal for the many portages, places where the canoes had to be carried on the paddlers' shoulders from waterway to waterway. In such canoes, paddlers could travel from fifty to seventy kilometres a day, including portages.

▲ **The cedar canoe.**
The Aboriginal Peoples of the West coast developed sturdy canoes carved from the trunks of great cedar trees. The canoes of the Haida people were large enough to carry many paddlers on expeditions in the open ocean. The high prow on the canoe allowed it to plow through the high waves of the Pacific Ocean.

▲ A voyageur canoe.

When European explorers, missionaries, and settlers arrived in Canada, they learned from the Aboriginal Peoples that the best way to get about was by canoe. They also learned how to construct canoes, how to paddle them, and the best routes to use in their exploration of much of the interior of the continent.

Later, great freight canoes paddled by *voyageurs* carried trade goods such as furs across the land. The largest of these canoes, the *canot du maître*, carried up to twelve paddlers, was twelve metres long, and could carry a 2300-kilogram load.

The voyageurs' network of waterways, supply stations, and portages reached from Montreal to Hudson Bay and to the Rocky Mountains. These routes would later form the basis for the highway and railway routes we use today.

But not all of the land could be travelled by canoe . . .

On the western plains, the Aboriginal Peoples used a type of sledge called a *travois* to carry goods from camp to camp. For the Inuit, the sled was an ideal means of getting over the snow and ice.

▲ A horse travois.
The travois is a sledge made of a platform or netting supported by two trailing poles. At one time, dogs were used to pull the travois. Later, horses were used because they could pull heavier loads.

▼ An Inuit dogsled.
Inuit sleds were made from wood, ivory, whalebone, or antlers. The runners were coated with ice or whale blubber to make them run smoothly. Sled dogs, bred by the Inuit, were strong enough to pull heavy loads for days at a time.

On the Atlantic coast, a different kind of water transport became important. Shipbuilding is one of Canada's oldest industries. In the latter part of the nineteenth century, shipyards throughout the Maritimes were a bustle of activity as many famous sailing ships were built. Canadian sailing ships were popular for their speed, great size, and good design. Eventually, however, iron-hulled steamships replaced the great wooden sailing ships.

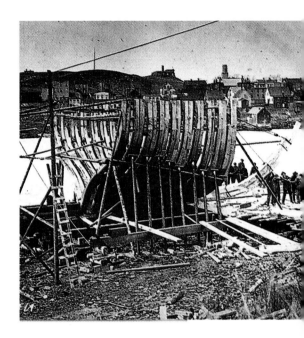

▲ **A sailing ship under construction.**

▲ **The *Marco Polo*.**

One of the most famous sailing ships was the Marco Polo, built at Saint John, New Brunswick, in 1851. On its first voyage it crossed the Atlantic Ocean in just sixteen days, an amazing feat in those days. For a time it was considered the fastest ship in the world.

The *Bluenose*. ▶
The schooner Bluenose, Canada's most famous sailing ship, was first launched at Lunenburg, Nova Scotia, in 1921. Between then and 1938, it won many sailing races, including the championship of the North Atlantic fishing fleets. If you look at a dime, you will see the image of the Bluenose. It also appears on stamps and many other items.

In early Canada, people did not have smooth paved highways. Roads were often little more than trails or wagon paths, rutted and bumpy. When it rained, they became mired in mud. Winter snows often blocked them completely. In many areas there were no roads at all. Settlers needed to be both hardy and ingenious when it came to getting around.

▲ **Cariboo stagecoach.**
These stagecoaches carried passengers, freight, gold, and mail through northern British Columbia. At times the ride was so rough that passengers suffered broken bones!

▲ **A Red River cart.**
The Red River cart was first used by the Métis, people of French and Aboriginal ancestry. They first used the carts to bring in meat from buffalo hunts. Later, they used them as farm carts. The Red River cart was made wholly of wood tied together with leather. It was easy to repair and very suitable for prairie conditions. Its high wheels made it stable, and it could be pulled through mud. Most important of all, it could carry loads as heavy as 450 kilograms.

▲ **A horse-drawn sleigh.**
A team of horses uses sleigh-runners to pull a load of lumber out of the woods.

The building of railways was an important step in linking the regions of Canada. The first railway, only twenty-two kilometres long, was built in the Montreal area in 1836. Before too long, however, railway lines grew across the land. One of the most important ever built was the Canadian Pacific Railway linking British Columbia and the rest of the nation. The construction of the railway was a daunting task, for track had to be laid across the rocks and forests of Ontario, across the prairies, and through the narrow mountain passes. Thousands of workers were needed. It took five long years, but in 1885, the last spike was driven in, linking the eastern and western sections of the railway.

▼ **Chinese railway workers.**
Over fifteen thousand Chinese immigrants came to Canada to work on the building of the Canadian Pacific Railway. Though they were industrious, steady workers, they were paid only half the wage of other workers, and were often given the most dangerous jobs, such as setting dynamite charges. At least six hundred of them died, many in dynamite blasts. Many more were injured, and received no compensation.

▲ **Driving the last spike.**
The ceremony took place on November 7, 1885. This has been called the most famous photo in Canadian history.

MEN WANTED!

A number of Men will be wanted by the undersigned during the grading season this year on west end of CANADIAN PACIFIC RAILWAY. Wages will be

$1.50 PER DAY,
BOARD $4.50 PER WEEK,

During the Summer Months for good, able-bodied, steady men.

Apply on the work at end of track. now near Cypress Hills. about 600 miles west of Winnipeg.

LANGDON, SHEPARD & CO., CONTRACTORS

▶ **Red Letter Day.**
This poster advertises the first passenger train leaving Montreal, Ottawa, and Toronto for the Pacific Coast.

Red Letter Day
For Canada
June 28, '86
CANADIAN PACIFIC
RAILWAY
OPENS PACIFIC OCEAN
TRAIN LEAVES DAILY:
Toronto, - - 5.00 p.m.
Montreal, - - 8.00 "
Ottawa, - - 11.45 "
OUR OWN LINE
ATLANTIC TO PACIFIC

As Canada moved into the twentieth century, adventurous and well-off Canadians traded in their horses and carriages for the automobile. Early motorists faced daunting problems. Breakdowns were frequent, and no driver went out without a well-equipped tool box. Then there were flat tires, dusty roads, and having to share the roads with horses. In Ontario, the early speed limit was seven miles per hour within one hundred yards of a horse! But before too many years had passed, the car had replaced the horse, and most Canadians have been zooming around the country in cars ever since. For some, even that wasn't fast enough. Fascinated by early airplanes, many Canadians became pioneers in the growth of aviation.

▲ **Advertisement for a Canadian car.**

▲ **Early automobile accident.**
As traffic increased, so did the number of automobile accidents. This one happened in Vancouver, British Columbia.

▼ **A sketch of the first snowmobile.**
Armand Bombardier built the first snowmobile in Quebec in 1926. It was made from a sleigh, an automobile engine, and an airplane propeller. In Canada's North today, snowmobiles carry people and goods where no other vehicles can go. Many of Canada's Inuit Peoples use skidoos and larger snowmobiles now instead of their traditional sleds.

▲ **The *Silver Dart.***
The first aircraft flight in Canada occurred in the winter of 1909 when the Silver Dart took off from the frozen bay of Baddeck, Nova Scotia.

Orangedale Whistle

by *Jimmy Rankin*
Illustrated by *Alain Massicotte*

The station master looked all around
Along the track both up and down
But the train could not be found
For there was neither sight nor sound
There was neither sight nor sound

He walked on slowly to the station door
Like so many times before
He looked outside into a sunshine beam
Closed his eyes and dreamed a dream
Drifted off into a dream

The winds of change forever grow
Some things stay and some things go
The falling rain must melt the snow
The Orangedale whistle will always blow

Years ago throughout this land
That line was laid by able men
But things saw change as time went by
Now people drive and people fly
Now people drive and people fly

The station master has long since gone
He faded off into the sun
But the whistle shrill still lingers on
In the hearts of everyone
Everyday from dusk 'till dawn

The winds of change forever grow
Some things stay and some things go
The falling rain must melt the snow
The Orangedale whistle will always blow

ABOUT THE AUTHOR   JIMMY RANKIN

Jimmy Rankin is a lead vocalist, guitar player, and primary songwriter for the *Rankin Family Band*. In crafting a song, Jimmy draws on a mix of pop, folk, and Celtic influences as well as his art college training. He says, "I am inspired by the basics . . . love, fate . . . whatever is striking about something I've seen or experienced." "Orangedale Whistle" was written in honor of the restoration of the Orangedale Train Station in Cape Breton. Jimmy's great-granduncle, Jim McFarlane, was the first Orangedale Station Master. The song was this successful band's first top-ten hit.

Silver Threads

by Marsha Forchuk Skrypuch
Illustrated by Michael Martchenko

In a land called Bukovyna, in Ukraine, a husband and wife farmed their narrow strip of land. Each morning, Ivan strapped the plough to his shoulders while Anna guided the plough through the rich black furrows of soil. "It takes two of us," Ivan would say, "one to push the plough and one to pull."

One afternoon, Ivan stopped in his tracks. "What's that sound?" he asked, frowning.

"Shouts," said Anna. "From the village!"

Ivan threw aside the plough straps and they raced to a hill that overlooked the village square. Hidden behind a tree, Anna and Ivan watched in horror as soldiers chained the village men and marched them away.

Anna and Ivan ran home.

The old woman who lived next door hobbled toward them. "Put this on," she told Ivan. "The soldiers will soon be back!" She threw a babushka, or granny shawl, over his shoulders.

"What does the foreign emperor want now?" Ivan asked.

"He needs more soldiers to help him steal other lands as he has stolen ours," she explained.

Ivan pushed the babushka away. "I will not fight for this emperor, but I am not a coward who will hide from the soldiers!"

"But what else can we do?" Anna asked.

"There is another way," said the woman. "A sign was posted in the village last month. It told of a country called 'Canada' across the ocean. It is a land of milk and honey with plenty of black soil but not enough farmers to plough it. One hundred and sixty acres are waiting for anyone brave enough to claim them."

One hundred and sixty acres of land? It seemed impossible! After all, Ivan and Anna's farm was a mere two acres. "Let us go, Ivan!" Anna cried. "We could plough those fields together."

That night, Ivan removed the one pane of glass from their small house and wrapped it in the babushka. Anna took the hinges from their door. They were ready to leave. "Wait," Ivan said. "One more thing!"

He walked to the corner of the house where a small black spider

spun a long silvery thread and wove it into a beautiful web. "Little spider, this will be the last time that I can feed you," he said, "but now is when we will need your good luck most of all." He sprinkled a few bread crumbs in front of the web, and in the darkness Anna and Ivan left their home.

With tears in their eyes, Anna and Ivan travelled across the ocean to Canada. The ship overflowed with people. As it tossed about on the waves, the two found refuge on a slat of wood in a dark corner. For company, there was a small spider who slowly spun out its web, unaware of the rollicking sea.

When the ship landed, Ivan and Anna found their journey was far from over. This part of Canada had no land to spare for newcomers. With the others from their ship, they travelled by train for days over the vast flat country.

The new soil was indeed black and rich as the sign had promised. But what the sign hadn't said was that the land was covered with trees. And that the winters were so cold a flask of water could freeze before it reached the lips.

But Anna and Ivan were happy.

They built a one-room home with a sod roof amid the wilderness. The pane of glass from the old country served as their one window. The hinges opened and closed their new door. And a tiny black spider nestled in a corner spinning its threads of silver. Though food was scarce, Ivan always found a few crumbs to share.

The thousands of trees that covered their land had to be removed one by one. It was backbreaking work, but Anna and Ivan didn't mind. After all, there were two of them, one to push the saw and one to pull. By spring, Ivan and Anna had sawed down three acres of trees. They traded the freshly cut wood for sacks of food.

Next, Ivan and Anna began the difficult job of removing the tree stumps from the newly thawed ground. By planting time, a single acre had been cleared. Shedding tears of pride, they planted their first small crop of wheat.

Though they were miles from the nearest village, their door was always open to those who travelled across the country to claim farms of their own. Thus it happened that one day they heard that Canada too had gone to war against the foreign emperor. Ivan leaped to his feet. "I could not save Bukovyna, but Canada is my country now. And I must fight."

Their last night together was Sviat Vechir—Christmas Eve. With a heavy heart, Anna scrubbed the table, and covered it with the freshly washed babushka. She prepared the meatless dishes, then counted to make sure she had the traditional twelve.

She set a sheaf of wheat—a didukh—in the corner of the room. Then together, she and Ivan cut a fir tree. It was not a difficult job for two— one to push the saw and the other to pull.

Ivan decorated the tree with cookies and a few shiny apples. But the festive house made them feel even sadder. Quietly, Anna helped her husband pack his bag. Early Christmas morning, they walked hand in hand to the distant village so that Ivan could enlist as a soldier.

"It will be hard for you to run the homestead by yourself," he told Anna. "You can push, but I won't be there to pull."

"I'll manage somehow," she said, firmly squeezing his hand.

They approached the town hall, passing a group of prisoners in chains. "Don't go in there!" one of the prisoners called to them in their own language. But Anna and Ivan ignored them.

A barrel-bellied official sat behind a desk. He glared at Ivan. "What do you want?"

"I want to fight for Canada. For my country," said Ivan, straightening his back.

"Your country?" cried the man. "You don't sound like a Canadian!"

"I was born in Bukovyna, Ukraine," said Ivan proudly, "but my country is Canada."

"You lie!" declared the official, rising. "Bukovyna is part of the Emperor's land. You are an enemy of Canada!"

"The Emperor stole Bukovyna from Ukraine!" Anna cried.

The official didn't listen. He shackled Ivan's wrists and dragged him to where the other prisoners were chained.

"Go home!" Ivan called to Anna. "Protect our homestead. We'll share another Sviat Vechir! I promise!"

Anna cried herself to sleep that night, wrapped in the babushka for warmth. The house was so silent. So still.

When she opened her eyes the next day, a bit of light was shining through the pane of glass. In the corner of the window, sparkling in the light, was a silver web made by Ivan's black spider.

Now, Anna was afraid of spiders, but in her loneliness, she was grateful for its company. Just as Ivan had done, she made sure the spider always had a few crumbs of bread in front of its web.

Without Ivan to help her, she couldn't cut down any more trees or remove any more stumps. She planted wheat in the acre of cleared soil, and vegetables around the stumps. Years passed with no word from her husband. Her store of food got smaller. As each Sviat Vechir came and went, Anna found herself alone.

She refused to give up hope, remembering Ivan's last words to her: "We'll share another Sviat Vechir! I promise!"

But one year, before the first snowflakes of winter fell to the ground, there was a knock that rattled the hinges of Anna's door.

It was the same government official who had put Ivan in chains! "You'll have to give up your homestead," he said, eyeing the farm with a gleam in his eye. "Your agreement says that you must clear some land each year and you haven't done that."

"But you took my husband away!" Anna cried. "I cannot clear it myself!"

"Don't you know the war has ended?" he asked. Then he folded his arms over his belly and added, "If your husband isn't home by now, he must be dead."

This was too much for Anna. She slumped on the doorstep and cradled her head in her hands.

The man's expression softened. "Well, I suppose I could give you

until next spring." Anna worked busily that autumn, bringing in her scanty harvest. The crop of wheat was poor, but she cut it anyway, and ground it between two stones to make coarse flour.

As Christmas approached, she still had not heard from Ivan. "I know in my heart that he is alive," she told the spider.

She swept the house thoroughly, making sure not to disturb the spider's web. Then she washed the walls and laundered the babushka and spread it on the scrubbed table. She looked at her thin store of food.

"Hmmm," she said. "It will take imagination to make the traditional twelve dishes from this!"

But she set to work, making a spoonful of the grain pudding known as kutia, two pyrohy, and two holubtsi, or cabbage rolls. She had one beet, so she made a cup of borscht. With her last bit of flour she made a tiny braided kolach. "Each mouthful will have to count as a dish," she mused.

She searched the field for what scattered stalks of wheat were left and bound them into a tiny didukh. She placed it in the corner. And then she set the table for two.

Suddenly she realized that she had no Christmas tree! Alone, she cut a fir and dragged it back to the house. It was hard work for one person. She could push the saw, but Ivan wasn't there to pull it.

She planted the tree in the dirt floor in front of the window and regarded it sadly. There was no flour left to make even one cookie to decorate it.

She lit a candle end and set that before the pane of glass, hoping that somehow, its light would guide Ivan home.

As the first star appeared, Anna prayed for her husband's return. She sat alone at the table set for two and waited.

But Ivan did not come. The candle spluttered and died. Anna couldn't bring herself to eat even a bite of the cold food. Shivering, she pulled the babushka from the table and wrapped herself in it, then cried herself to sleep.

Finally the sun shining through the window warmed her cheek. Her heart was so full of despair that she was afraid to open her eyes. She thought of the cold food, the bare tree, and the empty house. With a sigh, she rose.

She gazed at the light streaming through the window and drew a breath in wonder. The forlorn tree had been transformed, dazzling in a tapestry of silvery threads. On the topmost branch, the black spider slept, resting from an evening of labor.

The hinges of the door creaked. Anna turned and . . . there stood Ivan, tired, but alive!

She ran to the door and wrapped her arms around her husband. "You've come home!"

"I promised you I would," said Ivan, holding her tight. "And I did."

"But the war ended months ago," cried Anna.

"I escaped from the internment camp," he said, "and hid in the woods. I just heard that the war has ended." He gazed at the silvered fir tree. "This is what I saw through the window!" he exclaimed. "I was lost in the dark, then I noticed something sparkling in the distance. If it weren't for those silver threads, I might still be searching for home."

So Anna and Ivan had a joyous Sviat Vechir, even if the food was cold and a day late.

Now that there were two of them, they cleared the rest of the stumps in the first spring thaw. When the official returned, he was amazed at their progress.

"She pushes and I pull," Ivan explained. And his hand was firmly clasped in Anna's.

Historical Note

Between 1891 and 1914, thousands of Ukrainians, including my own grandparents, packed up their bags and moved to Canada.

These people were poor farmers of peasant stock who had little to look forward to if they stayed in their homeland. The average farm was two acres—barely enough to feed a family. And their part of Ukraine was occupied by the Austro-Hungarian Empire.

The Empire wished to take over more countries, so Ukrainians were rounded up and sent to fight the Empire's battles.

At this same time, Ottawa was looking for a way to clear and "populate" the vast Canadian prairies. Ukrainians were well known for their hard work and farming skills, so our government encouraged their emigration. Many Ukrainians were thrilled with this opportunity—the chance to come to Canada. It seemed like a dream come true.

When World War I broke out in 1914, Canada went to war against the German and Austro-Hungarian Empires. Even though our government had lured Ukrainians to come here with promises of freedom, these newcomers suddenly found themselves declared "enemy aliens" and many were imprisoned in concentration camps.

Approximately 5000 men, women, and children (some of whom had been born in Canada) were imprisoned between 1914 and 1920. The prisoners had their property and valuables taken away from them. To this day, much of this wealth has not been returned.

– *Marsha Forchuk Skrypuch*

ABOUT THE AUTHOR

MARSHA FORCHUK SKRYPUCH

Marsha Forchuk Skrypuch has wanted to be a writer ever since she was nine years old. She was inspired to write *Silver Threads* because her own grandfather was one of the thousands of people interned during World War I as an enemy alien. *Silver Threads* is her first book, but she has written hundreds of book reviews and articles for local newspapers and a magazine. Marsha lives in Brantford, Ontario, with her husband, Orest, her son, Neil, and her dog, Pepper.

Departure

As I looked back at my home
Tears rolled down my soft cheeks.
Yet, my tears were full of joy.

We were leaving for a new home,
For better opportunities.
We then set sail for our destination.

On arrival, my old uncle stood there
Waiting on the long shore,
Then I thought to myself, I am home.

I did miss my old home,
But the friendly atmosphere
Relieved me of my sorrows.

Aaron Haddad
Grade 6

Writing is like poetry. When I write, I always make sure that the story is flowing and has no incomplete thoughts.

Aaron Haddad

How My Family Came to Canada

My great-grandmother Lilian Swifte came to Canada from England in the early 1920s. She was in her twenties then. Her fiancé (who was in his twenties also) had already moved to British Columbia and was working to make enough money to bring Lilian to Canada so they could be married. So a few years after he moved to BC he had made enough money to bring Lilian to Canada. The arrangements were made for her to go on board the ship at 7:00 a.m. sharp on a Sunday. With a final goodbye to her family and friends, she was off. But on the ship she met an Irish man named James Swifte who was also going to Canada. They had a shipboard romance. A few short days before they arrived in Canada, James asked for her hand in marriage. Lilian said yes. When they arrived in Canada, Lilian told her other fiancé her decision. After that she worked as a maid in the fancy houses where she was living at the time. Lilian worked as a maid for a year. After that she moved to Selkirk and trained to be a nurse at the Selkirk Mental Health Centre, where my mom works today. After she trained for three years, Lilian and James were married. James was working at the Headingley Jail as a guard. A year after they got married, they had a son named John Allan Swifte. Lilian went back to England for a visit in 1964. That is how my family came to Canada.

Erin McElroy
Age 10

I wrote about this because it is an interesting part of my family history, and because we live in Selkirk, where Lilian and James were married.

Erin McElroy

Student Writing

From My Past

In 1850, my ancestor, Ambrose Aulenbach, came to Canada with my relatives and landed in Newfoundland. In 1950, they came to Manitoba. Ambrose Aulenbach was my great-great-great grandfather. They changed my last name from Aulenbach to Aulenback because the Canadians did not pronounce it with the "h". My last name means "brook that runs through the alders." The "Aulen" means "brook" in German and the "bach" means "alder"—a bush that grows in Germany. My grandpa says it is nice there and some day I would like to fly there and meet my cousins.

Robert Aulenback
Grade 5

The Smith Family

In 1905, a Smith family came to Alberta from the United States and settled in Westlock. It was a hard life for the Smiths because they were homesteading a half section of land and farming was hard to do.

The Smith family was generous. When families came and had little money, the Smiths took them in because they knew it was hard when you came. This was the beginning of friendships. Because of their generosity, they made lots of friends.

The Smith family enjoyed dances and picnics. First several people would start to sing and in the middle of the dance, people would start playing their guitars, fiddles, and pianos. These parties lasted all night because the Smiths and other families had so much fun that they lost track of time.

I am proud to come from a family that is respected and that helped build Alberta's history.

Amanda Smith
Age 10

The Lotus Seed

by Sherry Garland

Illustrated by Tatsuro Kiuchi

My grandmother saw
the emperor cry
the day he lost
his golden dragon throne.

She wanted something
to remember him by,
so she snuck down
to the silent palace,
near the River of Perfumes,
and plucked a seed
from a lotus pod
that rattled
in the Imperial garden.

She hid the seed
in a special place
under the family altar,
wrapped in a piece of silk
from the *ao dai*
she wore that day.
Whenever she felt sad
or lonely,
she took out the seed
and thought of the
brave young emperor.

And when she married
a young man
chosen by her parents,
she carried the seed
inside her pocket
for good luck, long life,
and many children.
When her husband
marched off to war,
she raised her
children alone.

One day bombs fell
all around,
and soldiers
clamored door to door.
She took the time
to grab the seed,
but left her mother-of-pearl
hair combs lying
on the floor.

One terrible day
her family scrambled
into a crowded boat
and set out
on a stormy sea.
Bà watched the mountains
and the waving palms
slowly fade away.
She held the seed
in her shaking fingers
and silently said goodbye.

She arrived in a
strange new land
with blinking lights
and speeding cars
and towering buildings
that scraped the sky
and a language
she didn't understand.

She worked many years,
day and night,
and so did her children
and her sisters
and her cousins, too,
living together
in one big house.

Last summer
my little brother
found the special seed
and asked questions
again and again.
He'd never seen a lotus bloom
or an emperor
on a golden dragon throne.

So one night
he stole the seed
from beneath the family altar
and planted it
in a pool of mud
somewhere near Bà's
onion patch.

Bà cried and cried
when she found out
the seed was gone.
She didn't eat,
she didn't sleep,
and my silly brother
forgot what spot of earth
held the seed.

Then one day in spring
my grandmother shouted,
and we all ran
to the garden
and saw
a beautiful pink lotus
unfurling its petals,
so creamy and soft.

"It is the flower
of life and hope,"
my grandmother said.
"No matter how ugly the mud
or how long the seed lies
dormant,
the bloom will be beautiful.
It is the flower
of my country."

When the lotus blossom
faded and turned
into a pod,
Bà gave each of
her grandchildren
a seed
to remember her by,
and she kept one
for herself
to remember the emperor by.

I wrapped my seed
in a piece of silk
and hid it
in a secret place.
Someday I will plant it
and give the seeds
to my own children
and tell them about the day
my grandmother saw
the emperor cry.

Author's Note

For centuries, emperors ruled Vietnam with absolute power because the people believed they were messengers from heaven, and all-wise. One emperor built a magnificent palace on the River of Perfumes in the city of Hue, surrounded by majestic mountains. Modelled after the famous Forbidden City in Peking, China, it was a city within a city, filled with fantastic gardens and orchards and surrounded by lotus-filled moats. Elaborate gates and graceful bridges crossed the moats to the part of Hue where the ordinary citizens lived.

In the late 1800s, France conquered Vietnam and made it into a colony. The French exploited the land and people, and soon the emperors lost their power. The last emperor of Vietnam, Nguyen Vinh Thuy, was born in 1913. When he took the throne at the age of twelve, he became Bao Dai, "Keeper of Greatness." Although he had no real power, Bao Dai was a symbol of Vietnamese heritage and he performed at traditional ceremonies.

Many Vietnamese wanted to be free of French rule and become an independent nation again. So, in 1945, Bao Dai abdicated his throne, handing over his golden seal and golden sword to leaders of the independence movement led by Ho Chi Minh. A bloody war followed, until 1954, when Vietnam defeated the French and won its independence at last.

But Vietnam was still a country in turmoil and soon another war erupted between the north and south. This time the United States helped the southerners. The civil war lasted until 1975, when the south was defeated.

As the conquering northern armies swept down, about one million Vietnamese fled by way of boat. They came from all walks of life—teachers, doctors, merchants, farmers, fishermen— leaving behind their homes, possessions, families, and friends. America became the new home for the majority of Vietnamese refugees.

ABOUT THE AUTHOR   SHERRY GARLAND

Award-winning author Sherry Garland had her first success as an author when she entered and won an essay contest at age seventeen. After that experience, she "dreamed of being an author." Fifteen years later she began writing paperbacks for adults. In 1988 Sherry wrote her first book for young people. She says that she discovered that she "loves writing fiction for children of all ages from the very young readers of picture books to middle grade readers and young adults."

ROOTS

Ancestry

by Ashley Bryan
Illustrated by Stephen Taylor

I splash in the ocean
My big brother watches me
We sing,
"Wade in the water
Wade in the water, children."

Mom and Dad
Teaching us spirituals
Reading us African tales
Singing songs
Telling stories
Reminding us
Of our ancestry

On the beach
Other children
Dig to China
I dig
To Africa

Family Gifts

by Victor Cockburn and Judith Steinbergh
Illustrated by Leon Zernitsky

Grandma stitched a special quilt,
She smoothed it on her bed,
And wore it 'round her shoulders.
Then one day my grandma said . . .
Here's a special present,
A quilt to bring you sleep,
I hope it makes you warm and safe,
A gift you'll always keep.

CHORUS

Gifts of rings and patchwork,
Coins and recipes,
Pumpkin pies and lullabies,
Will bind our families.

Aunt Rose has an armchair
With saggy saggy springs.
Its stuffing fluffs into the air
Like puffs of pigeon wings.
"Would you like this armchair?"
Our Aunt Rose said one day,
"You will have a place to rest
When I have moved away."

CHORUS

Grandpa came from Russia,
He brought a coin with him,
A coin his dad had given,
He sewed it in his hem.
He always rubbed it in his hand,
Until the picture blurred,
One day he slipped it in my palm
And didn't say a word.

CHORUS

I Grew Up

by Lenore Keeshig-Tobias
Illustrated by Stephen Taylor

i grew up on the reserve
thinking it was the most
beautiful place in the world

i grew up thinking
i'm never going
to leave this place

i was a child
a child who would
lie under trees

watching wind's rhythms
sway leafy boughs
back and forth

back and forth
sweeping it seemed
the clouds into great piles

and rocking me as
i snuggled in the grass
like a bug basking in the sun

i grew up on the reserve
thinking it was the most
beautiful place in the world

i grew up thinking
i'm never going
to leave this place

i was a child
a child who ran
wild rhythms

through the fields
the streams
the bush

eating berries
cupping cool water
to my wild stained mouth

and hiding in the
treetops with
my friends

we used to laugh at teachers and
tourists who referred to
our bush as *forests* or *woods*

forests and *woods*
were places of
fairytale text

were places where people
especially children, got lost
where wild beasts roamed

our bush was where we played
and where the rabbits squirrels
foxes deer and the bear lived

i grew up thinking
i'm never going
to leave this place

i grew up on the reserve
thinking it was the most
beautiful place in the world

Our First Fast

by Sophia Mir
Illustrated by Taddeuz Majewski

Days of Ramadan begin before sunset, when we eat heaping plates and drink sugary tea.

Stomachs grumble and energy is low—our eyes are hungry in the late afternoon.

But the sun sets as it always does. We look for the crescent moon in the sky. Our mom has made our favorite dishes, the smells from the kitchen make our stomachs talk.

We bite into our Medina dates and sip the Zamzam water. We think of those who don't have what we have, and we whisper, in God's Ear, our thanks.

We fasted our first fast and we laugh and kid because we are proud.

"Happy Ramadan," our parents smile.

The Sacred Harvest

by Gordon Regguinti
Photographed by Dale Kakkak

Wild rice, which the Ojibwa call mahnomin (mah-NO-men), *has long been an important food for Native Americans in the Upper Great Lakes region. Archaeologists say that Indians gathered wild rice as far back as 2500 years ago.*

For the Ojibwa, wild rice is not only a basic food crop, it also has spiritual meaning. Stories have been handed down that tell of a time when the Ojibwa lived on the East Coast. Prophets spoke of a great journey the Ojibwa people must make if they were to survive. The journey would end in a land where food grew abundantly in the water. This place would be their home, and the food a gift of the Creator.

The migration took hundreds of years. Finally, in the mid-1500s, the Ojibwa found their special place in what is now northern Minnesota and Wisconsin. Wild rice became a staple of their diet, helping them survive the cold, harsh winters.

Wild rice has been called the perfect food. It is high in protein, carbohydrates, and fibre, but low in fat. Actually, it is not a true rice like white rice, but a grain that grows on top of a long grass.

The Upper Great Lakes region is one of the few places where wild rice grows naturally. It needs rivers and lakes with muddy bottoms, where the soil is stirred so seeds get the oxygen and nutrients they need to sprout. This stirring happens when snow and ice melt in the spring, causing flooding.

In late April, when the lakes and rivers warm up, the seeds sprout and anchor their roots into the newly stirred soil. Then the plants begin to grow, drawing food from the rich soil and energy from the sun. Finally, during the warm days and cool nights of late August and early September, the plants ripen, and their grains are ready to be gathered.

Eleven-year-old Glen Jackson had waited for this day all year. It was the first time his father would take him out to gather mahnomin, the sacred food of the Ojibwa people. This was the day he would become a wild ricer. As they dragged the canoe down the narrow path toward the river, Glen wondered if he would be strong enough to push the boat through the thick wild rice bed.

The day was a good one for ricing. After only an hour, Glen and his father had filled the bottom of the canoe. They could hear other harvesters on the river, but the tall rice stalks hid them from view. Occasionally they spotted the tops of poles rising out of the rice bed.

Glen and his father developed a rhythm as they added rice to the pile. Every time the canoe slowed, Glen would quickly lift the pole from the water, slip it back in, and push off, keeping the boat moving smoothly. As the boat slid forward, his father reached over with one knocker and bent the rice stalks over the side of the canoe. He raised the other knocker and aimed for the tops of the stalks. *Swish!* The knockers sent rice grains flying into the canoe.

Soon it was Glen's turn to be the knocker. It took him some time to find his rhythm. Sometimes he barely got the rice over the canoe before it slipped from his grasp. Other times Glen gave a mighty swing but missed the rice altogether. His knocker crashed into the canoe, and a loud bang echoed across the river. Finally, after many tries, Glen began to bring in rice!

When the sun was high in the sky, Glen and his father made their way toward the landing. Onshore they unloaded their gear and

▼ *Packing.*

▲ *Harvesting.*

71

cleaned the rice. They had done well, harvesting over forty-five kilograms. They packed it into narrow sacks, careful not to spill any.

Glen and his parents headed for Grandmother's house to process the rice. When they arrived, they had many things to do before the rice would be ready to eat.

They dumped the rice onto a plastic tarp to dry. Glen's father brought out a large cast-iron kettle and set it at an angle against two iron poles. The kettle would be used to parch the rice, or loosen the grains from the husks by cooking out moisture.

▲ *Parching.*

▲ *Drying.*

While his father searched for firewood, Glen gathered kindling. Then they built a small fire underneath the kettle. When the kettle was hot, they put in some of the rice and took turns stirring it. Constant stirring kept the rice from burning and helped it cook evenly. When the husks turned golden brown and started separating from the grains, they poured the rice onto a tarp to cool. They repeated the process until all the rice was parched.

The next step was jigging or "dancing" on the rice to grind the husks away from the kernels. Glen's father changed into soft leather moccasins so he wouldn't crush the rice grains. He found a small

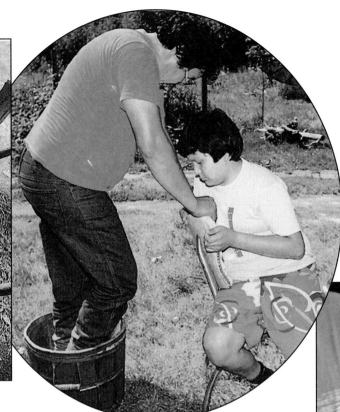

▲ *Husking.*

birchbark containers and lightly tossed it in the air. The wind blew the chaff away, and the heavier grains fell back into the container.

Finally enough rice was finished to make a meal. When Grandmother headed for the house with the finished rice, Glen knew he would soon be enjoying a taste of his first harvest.

wooden bucket, filled it about one-quarter full of parched rice, and began dancing on it.

Every so often he stopped and examined a handful of rice. When he could no longer see any husks attached to the grains, he took the rice out of the bucket and added more. This part of the process was slow and tiresome. After what seemed like hours, the jigging was complete.

The family then began the last step. The ground husks—called chaff—must be separated, or winnowed, from the rice. They dumped the rice into

▲ *Winnowing.*

▲ *Celebrating the harvest.*

Grandmother came outside carrying a pot of cooked wild rice. She spread a blanket on the ground and asked everyone to sit down.

Before they ate, Grandmother talked about Glen's first harvest. It was important for Glen to learn about his people's history and to know that rice meant survival to the Ojibwa. By harvesting rice, Glen could feel that he was a part of the natural world. Grandmother then asked the Creator to bless her grandson. Glen ate a spoonful of the wild rice. He loved its soft texture and sweet, nutty taste. It was delicious!

ABOUT THE AUTHOR   GORDON REGGUINTI

Gordon Regguinti is a member of the Leech Lake Band of Ojibway. He was raised on Leech Lake Reservation by his mother and grandparents. As a young man, Gordon began to harvest wild rice on Leech Lake. A graduate of the University of Minnesota with a degree in Indian Studies, he has written about Native Peoples issues for newspapers and educational programs. He is managing editor of *Colors*, a magazine for people of color.

We Are All Related

A Celebration of Our Cultural Heritage

by Students of G.T. Cunningham Elementary School

To me "We Are All Related" means that we are friends, respect one another, behave, and play safe.

I AM DEREK BULHOES

My family comes from Portugal.

The elders in this collage are grandpa and grandma (my dad's mother and father).

The photograph shows me with my dad holding me. I was three years old. I drew a fishing boat from an encyclopedia picture of Portugal found in our school library. People in Portugal do a lot of fishing. I like to fish too.

The border on my collage is a pattern of fish, a sun, and a triangle.

I thought they looked nice together.

I think this project was fun and interesting. I learned about Portugal and the importance of respecting each other. Other people can learn about different cultures by looking at the heritage collages.

The Elders Speak

"I would like young people to learn from me . . . to be helpful and not to be mean."

— *Noberto Bulhoes (Derek's dad)*

To me "We Are All Related" means that we are all connected. I learned that we should try to have balance in our lives and respect each other.

My family comes from Hong Kong. The elders in this collage are mom and dad.

The photograph shows me when I was six years old. I write Chinese words because they stand for our culture. The Chinese words in my collage mean: sun, moon, mountain, red, girl, boy, grandma, and grandpa.

The border on my collage is a pattern of suns, trees, and geometric shapes.

I enjoyed this project because placing the photographs was fun.

The Elders Speak

"I would like young people to learn from me . . . to listen to your elders and don't fight with your brother."

— Mei Va Kwan (Pauline's grandma)

76

*To me "We Are All Related" means that we are related in friendship and the bond
between us, because we are not all related by blood. Respect yourself
and the environment.*

I Am Robert Fox

I am a First Nations person. I am Northern Tutchone. My family comes from the Yukon Territory.

The elder in this collage is my grandmother, Effie.

The photograph shows me with my grandmother.

I drew a yin-yang symbol on my shirt because it stands for black and white, good and bad.

The border on my collage is a pattern of trees and buildings. It shows the separation of Mother Nature and civilization. The inner border symbolizes the Wolf Clan and the Crow Clan. I come from the Crow Clan.

I think this project was very educational because it taught kids about Aboriginal People.

The Elders Speak

"I would like young people to learn from me . . . to play sports, keep healthy, and not to watch TV anymore."

— Gordon Brunton (Robert's grandpa)

77

To me "We Are All Related" means that we are all connected. Live in peace.

I Am Cindy Mehat

My family comes from India.

The elders in this collage are my mommy, Sharnjit, and dad, Raminder Mehat.

I drew a line of dogs because they often help people in India. I had five dogs, when I stayed there.

My mommy is wearing a punjabi suit and the colors on her suit are dark pink, and black with golden diamonds. My daddy is wearing a man's suit and a tie. The suit is black and the tie is dark red and grey with a pattern.

The border on my collage is a pattern of suns, stars, boxes, and lines.

I think this project was excellent and fun because it taught me all about First Nations symbols. It is important to learn about different beliefs and different cultural symbols. By becoming more aware of these we can see that people have similar values and beliefs.

The Elders Speak

"I would like young people to learn from me . . . to respect others and not to smoke."

— *Raminder Mehat (Cindy's daddy)*

My Heritage

I'm Canadian, but in my blood I have Norwegian, French, English, and Scottish parts. I'm mostly Norwegian. At Christmas we open our presents on Christmas Eve. My family doesn't have turkey. We have spare ribs and "søt suppe." This is like fruit soup, with peaches, grapes, prunes, and apples. We also have rice pudding and "lefse," a very thin potato crêpe. On Christmas we go to the Lutheran church. In Norway the Lutheran church is the most common. When my mom was younger she went to Norway and stayed with my grandparents' relatives. My mom also learned Norwegian in university. She stayed there for one year. My name, my brother's name, and my cousins' names are very Norwegian. Their names are Erik, Nils, Olaf, Torbjorn, Annelise, and my name is Ingrid. Three of my grandparents are all Norwegian. Only one of my grandparents isn't Norwegian. He is French, English, and Scottish. That is my heritage.

Ingrid Parker
Age 11

Chinese Celebration

The Chinese people have a great celebration when Chinese New Year is here.

Unlike for western people, New Year's is in early to mid February for the Chinese. Everybody receives red pockets with money inside, just to celebrate a new year. Many people on New Year's Day go to a very special place to pray to the gods. They have three sticks, and bow three times.

There once was a story about a queen and twelve animals, which were the tiger, snake, mouse, dragon, rabbit, dog, sheep, ox, pig, horse, rooster, and the monkey. One day they were very bored, so the queen decided to have a competition on the next day. "Whoever gets here the earliest will represent the first year, and the second animal that comes will represent the second year, and the next animal will be the next, until the twelfth animal arrives," the queen said.

The first animal, to represent the first year, was the mouse. The second was the ox. The third was the tiger. The fourth was the rabbit, then the dragon, the snake, the horse, the sheep, the monkey, the rooster, the dog, and the pig. After all the animals have represented their year, the mouse starts again.

On New Year's Day you shouldn't talk about anything that is bad. You shouldn't say anything about death.

New Year's Day is a very happy thing to celebrate.

Dianna Lau
Grade 5

I like to write because I enjoy reading my own writing. Writing something is likable because it makes me proud of my writing. When I read a book that I enjoy, I always want to write as well as many authors do.

Dianna Lau

79

Navroz

"Navroz" is on the first day of Spring (March 21). It is the new year for Ismaili Muslims. "Navroz" means new year's day. It is a sign of a new beginning, birth and life. Since it is the first day of spring, it is the beginning of trees growing, flowers blooming, and animals having babies. Because it is the beginning of a new life cycle, we usually reflect on what we did the year before and try to keep the promises we make for the new year.

We usually take "Rozi," comprised of dried fruit, wheat, and sweets, to church. It symbolizes happiness and prosperity.

Navroz is a time of great rejoicing throughout the world for Ismailis. I look forward to this day because we exchange gifts and we have my favorite meal at home. My aunts and uncles phone from all over Canada to wish us a happy Navroz day!

Here is a poem for Navroz day:

Navroz is a rejoiceful day
A first day of spring
When trees begin to grow
Animals have babies
Farmers get ready to farm
Everybody prays for health and happiness

Salimah Kassamaili
Age 10

> For me, writing is difficult to start, but once I have started I see many opportunities or choices, and I can then write pages and pages.

Karl Torbicki

December Celebrations

As December approaches we prepare for the holidays we celebrate. Some celebrate Christmas, and others, Hanukkah. Our family celebrates Christmas. December makes us think of presents, gingerbread, Santa, sleds, snow, and candy. We get out wreaths, advent calendars, stockings, dradels, and Menorahs. Many people buy Christmas trees to decorate with colorful lights and bulbs. On Christmas Eve we are all kept awake by our hopes for many presents, and also by our dad's snoring. In the morning we spring from our beds and zip to the Christmas tree, hoping to see big presents rather than lumps of coal.

Karl Torbicki
Grade 6

Interview on Sikhism

There was a man named Bill who wanted to learn about different cultures. At a restaurant he saw a man sitting alone. He went and asked him some questions.

BILL: I saw you sitting here all by yourself. May I join you?

GURJOT SINGH: Sure, you can join me.

BILL: Let me introduce myself. My name is Bill.

GURJOT SINGH: And my name is Gurjot Singh.

BILL: I would like to ask you a few questions about you and your culture, if you don't mind. Where are you from?

GURJOT SINGH: I come from India.

BILL: So what religion are you?

GURJOT SINGH: I am a Sikh.

BILL: Most Sikhs wear turbans. Why do you?

GURJOT SINGH: It is to protect our hair, which is to be kept uncut.

BILL: I have heard of "5 K's." What are they?

GURJOT SINGH: The 5 K's are Kirpan, Kacchaara, Kara, Kesh, and Kanga. A Kirpan is a small sword. A Kacchaara is an undergarment. A Kara is a steel bracelet, and it means "God is one." Kesh is uncut hair. A Kanga is a small comb to keep your hair in place.

BILL: Oh, look at the time. I'm going to be late for my next meeting.

GURJOT SINGH: OK, see you next time. Bye, Bill.

Gurjit Flora
Age 10